# Specialties from the Southern Garden

*Nostalgic Vegetable Dishes*

Patricia B. Mitchell

Copyright © 1999 by Patricia B. Mitchell. All rights reserved.

Portions of this manuscript were previously published under the titles *Salad Days*, © 1992 by Patricia B. Mitchell, and *Southern Specialty Vegetables*, © 1992 by Patricia B. Mitchell.

Published 1999 by the author.
Mail: Mitchells, Box 429, Chatham, VA 24531
Book Sales: 800-967-2867
E-mail: *Answers@FoodHistory.com*
Websites: *FoodHistory.com* and *MitchellsPublications.com*

Compact Edition
Printed in the U.S.A.
ISBN-10: 0-925117-94-3
ISBN-13: 978-0-925117-94-6

Fourth Printing, May 2010

- *Illustrations* -

Front Cover – Adapted from a crayon drawing by Alice Barber Stephens, ca. 1917-18, created for a poster entitled "Somebody has to raise everything you eat — do your share," provided by the Library of Congress. The background is an image of a lettuce leaf.

Inside Title Page – Adapted from an image created by Howell Lithograph Company, Hamilton, Ontario, ca. 1914-18, for a poster entitled "Waste not, want not, prepare for winter: save perishable foods by preserving now," provided by the Library of Congress.

Back Cover – "A Spring Scene Near Richmond, Virginia," wood engraving by William Ludwell Sheppard, from *Harper's Weekly*, May 21, 1870, p. 321, provided by the Library of Congress.

Graphic research and design are by Sarah E. Mitchell, *VintageDesigns.com*.

# Table of Contents

**Introduction** ..... 1
   "... Almost Every Desirable Thing in Life ..." ..... 1
   The Early Southerner Gets the Vegetables ..... 1
**Aspiring to Asparagus** ..... 2
   Fresh-from-the-Garden Asparagus Spears ..... 3
   Mama's Reassuring Rice and Asparagus Casserole ..... 3
   A Belle's Golden Crown Casserole ..... 3
   The Corner A&P Casserole ..... 4
   B'burg C'burg Asparagus Newburg ..... 4
   Carolina Jewels Asparagus Salad ..... 5
**Aesthetics of Broccoli and Cauliflower** ..... 6
   Miss Southland Basic Broccoli ..... 6
   "Say Cheese" Sauce for Broccoli ..... 6
   Tennessee Beauty Broccoli Bake ..... 7
   Alabama Strut Broccoli Salad ..... 7
   Miss Congeniality Cauliflower Salad ..... 8
**Comforting Cabbage** ..... 8
   Southern Slope Cabbage Wedges ..... 9
   Summer Respite Ice Box Slaw ..... 9
   Smooth and Creamy Coleslaw ..... 10
   Taste of Texas Coleslaw ..... 10
   "Cabbage Boiled with Bacon" ..... 11
**All-Consumed Corn** ..... 11
   Summer Succulence Grilled Corn on the Cob ..... 11
   My Mama's Corn Pudding ..... 12
   Best-of-the-Patch Corn and Tomato Casserole ..... 12
   Cob's Legion Fresh Corn Fritters ..... 13
**The Long Lean String Bean** ..... 13
   Capital City Almond-Crowned Beans ..... 14
   Snaps Under Pressure ..... 14
   Southern-Style Pole Beans and New Potatoes ..... 14
   Quintessential Four Bean Salad ..... 15
   North Carolina Bean Salad ..... 15
**Lettuce, Pray** ..... 16
   Mrs. McGregor's Lettuce Salad ..... 16
**The Sublime Subliminal Lima** ..... 17
   "Lima Beans" ..... 17
   Cool Breezes Lima Salad ..... 17
**More than Merely Mushrooms** ..... 18
   Louisiana Mushroom Casserole ..... 18
**Summer-Sensing Okra** ..... 19
   Creole Okra ..... 19
**Of Onions and Spring** ..... 20
   Fried Spring Onions ..... 20

Simply Nice Green Rice ................................................................................20
Favorite Things Salad ..................................................................21
**The Honorable Black-Eyed Pea** ................................................................21
"Cornfield or Black Eye Peas" ...................................................21
"Recipe for Cooking Cornfield Peas" ........................................22
Outstanding Dried Black-Eyed Peas ..........................................22
**Soothing Potatoes** ......................................................................................23
Gravy-Sopping Mashed Potatoes ................................................23
". . . Variety in the Diet . . ." .....................................................23
"To Boil Irish Potatoes" ............................................................23
Neatly Parsleyed New Potatoes ..................................................24
Flatlanders' Pan-Fried Potatoes .................................................24
Old-Fashioned Cheese-Scalloped Potatoes ................................24
Not-Much-Trouble Scalloped Potatoes ......................................25
Portly Potatoes ...........................................................................25
Chill-Out Potato Salad ...............................................................26
**Garden Greens** ............................................................................................26
Family Spinach Salad .................................................................26
Southern Lady's Creamed Spinach ............................................27
Turnip Greens with Cornmeal Dumplings .................................27
Southern Classic Turnip Salad Greens ......................................28
**Prodigious Squash** ......................................................................................28
Home Kitchen Squash ................................................................28
"To Stew Cymlings (or Squash, as it is sometimes called)" ..........28
Ritzy Company Squash Casserole .............................................29
Savory Summer Squash .............................................................29
Church Supper Squash ...............................................................29
Happy Discovery Yellow Squash ...............................................30
**"Long" or Sweet Potatoes** ..........................................................................30
"To Boil Sweet Potatoes" ..........................................................30
Southern Sensations Fried Sweet Potatoes ................................31
Big Orange Mashed Sweet Potatoes ..........................................31
How Sweet They Are! ................................................................31
Cousin Kathy's Sweet Potato Casserole ....................................32
**A Vegetable by Any Other Name** .............................................................32
Green Tomato Casserole ............................................................33
"Stewed Tomatoes" ....................................................................33
Heavenly Halves Broiled Tomato Cups .....................................33
Cousin Tinky's Tomato Cheese Dumplings ...............................34
Pick of the Patch Tomato-Herb Salad ........................................34
Edenton Tomato Aspic ...............................................................35
**Conclusion** ..................................................................................................35
**Notes** ............................................................................................................35

# Introduction

## "... Almost Every Desirable Thing in Life..."

Southerners have been successful vegetable growers since even before the South was called "the South." In 1791 William Bartram, Philadelphia Quaker and natural scientist, wrote of his travels in the southern regions of the United States:

"... [B]y the arts of agriculture and commerce, almost every desirable thing in life might be produced and made plentiful here ... as this soil and climate appear to be of a favourable nature for the production of almost all the fruits of the earth ... corn, rice, and all the esculent vegetables." [1]

Raising and eating vegetables, or raising and preserving them for future use, have always been part of Southern culture, especially during hard times when meat was scarce. Wars, economic depressions, and poverty made many gardens "victory gardens" — victory over shortages and hunger. Homemakers reveled in their garden abundance, and in many cases dried, pickled, or canned their way to winter meal variety. Whether fresh or preserved, vegetables are, and have been, an expected part of a "square" Southern meal. This book contains some relic recipes from the 19th century, and some reminiscent recipes from earlier decades of the 20th century.

## The Early Southerner Gets the Vegetables

Marion Cabell Tyree, editor of *Housekeeping In Old Virginia*, which was published in 1879, advised:

"If possible, use vegetables gathered early in the morning, with the dew on them. . . . If you are living in the city, get your vegetables from market as early in the morning as possible.

"As soon as gathered or brought from market, all vegetables should be carefully picked over, washed, placed in fresh water, and set in a cool place till the cook is ready to put them on for dinner.

[Another authoress remarks, "If you live in the country, have your vegetables gathered from the garden at an early hour, so that there is ample time to make your search for caterpillars, &c." [2]]

"Put them on in water neither cold nor boiling hot. The slow heating that takes place when you put them on in cold water deprives them of their flavor, to some extent, whilst too rapid heating toughens the vegetable fibre.

"Just before they are thoroughly done and tender, add sufficient salt to season them. Do not stir them and mutilate them with a spoon, but turn them into a colander and drain. Place them in a hot dish and put a large tablespoonful of fresh butter over them.

"In cooking dried peas and beans, as well as corn put up in brine, always soak them . . . overnight. These vegetables should first be parboiled, whether they are to be used for soup or for side dishes." [3]

## Aspiring to Asparagus

Many old Southern homesites have a spot which sprouts asparagus (if the shoots are not harvested), gifts from a gardener of long ago. When my husband and I purchased our old house, we found asparagus *everywhere* on the property! In our youthful exuberance, we tried to move it all to a tidy symmetrical bed. A Southern summer drought intervened, and, alas, our cherished asparagus was no more!

Asparagus is superb lightly steamed and *devoured.* Or, for a refreshing variation, we like to chill the cooked asparagus and serve with blue cheese dressing. If fresh asparagus cannot be had, one can simply open a can of asparagus, drain, and serve on lettuce leaves with dressing. Another alternative would be to use one of the following recipes to satisfy that asparagus craving.

# Fresh-from-the-Garden Asparagus Spears

2½ - 3 lbs. fresh asparagus
1 c. water
2 - 4 tbsp. butter, melted
Pimiento strips

    Wash the asparagus, and break off the tough ends of stems at the point where they are brittle. Place in boiling, salted water to cover, and simmer 10-15 minutes or until tender. Arrange the cooked spears on a warmed serving platter, and pour the melted butter over them. Garnish with pimiento strips. Serves 6 to 8.


# Mama's Reassuring Rice and Asparagus Casserole

3 c. hot cooked rice
1 c. sharp Cheddar cheese, grated
1 can asparagus spears (*or* 2 c. fresh asparagus, cooked until just tender)
1 (10½ oz.) can cream of mushroom soup

    Spoon half the rice into a buttered 2-quart casserole dish. Sprinkle with ½ c. cheese; repeat with remaining rice and cheese. Drain asparagus, reserving liquid. Arrange asparagus over all. Blend asparagus liquid and soup. Pour over casserole. Bake at 350° F. for 30 minutes. Yield: 4 to 6 servings.[4]


# A Belle's Golden Crown Casserole

Ritz crackers
1 (10 oz.) pkg. frozen green peas (*or* 2 c. fresh shelled green peas)
1 (10½ oz.) can cream of mushroom soup
1 can asparagus (undrained), *or* 2 c. fresh asparagus (cooked until just tender)
Canned French-fried onion rings, grated Cheddar cheese, *or* sliced hard-cooked eggs

Line a round Pyrex baking bowl or dish with Ritz crackers, allowing the crackers to form a crown-like ring around the upper edge. Cook quite briefly the peas in a tiny amount of boiling water. (Almost every drop of the water should cook away.) To the green peas add the soup and asparagus. Mix and spoon into the cracker-lined baking dish. Bake at 350° F. until bubbly (20-30 minutes). Cover with canned onion rings, Cheddar cheese, or sliced hard-cooked eggs. (The yellow of the eggs or cheese is really beautiful!) Heat 5 additional minutes. Yield: approximately 6 servings.[5]

## The Corner A&P Casserole

When my husband and I lived at 612 Royal Street, New Orleans, the A&P was just a short half-block away, on the corner of Royal and St. Peter. It provided all our garden succulents (including the Asparagus & Peas).

\* \* \*

1 (10½ oz.) can asparagus (*or* 2 c. fresh, lightly-cooked asparagus)
1 (8½ oz.) can tiny peas (*or* 1 c. fresh shelled peas)
1 (8 oz.) can sliced water chestnuts
1 (10½ oz.) can cream of mushroom soup
½ c. sharp Cheddar cheese, grated
Buttered bread crumbs

Drain the vegetables. Make layers of veggies, soup, and cheese in a casserole dish. Bake at 325° F. for 25 minutes. Then top with additional cheese and crumbs and bake 5 to 10 minutes more.

## B'burg-C'burg Asparagus Newburg

Our college days and first year of marriage (and recipe-collecting) were spent in then-tiny Blacksburg, Virginia, just over the hill from also-small Christiansburg.

\* \* \*

3/4 lb. fresh asparagus
1 1/2 c. boiling water
1/4 tsp. salt (or to suit taste)
1/2 c. sliced almonds
3 tbsp. butter *or* margarine
2 tbsp. all-purpose flour
1/2 c. milk
1 c. sliced fresh mushrooms
1 tsp. cooking sherry
Toast

Clean asparagus for cooking. Trim woody fiber from broken-off tough ends, cut in 1-inch lengths, and place in a saucepan. Add water and salt; boil uncovered for 15 to 18 minutes. Add heads after the first 8 minutes of cooking. Meanwhile, sauté almonds in heated butter for a few minutes until golden brown. Do not scorch. Stir flour into butter-almond mixture until well blended. Add milk gradually. Cook over medium heat until sauce boils and thickens, stirring to keep smooth. Blend in undrained asparagus, mushrooms, and sherry carefully. Cover and simmer for 10 minutes, stirring occasionally. Serve over toast squares. Yield: 4 servings.

## Carolina Jewels Asparagus Salad

3/4 c. sugar
1 c. water (use liquid from canned asparagus, adding water to equal one cup of liquid)
1/2 c. white vinegar or apple cider vinegar
2 tbsp. gelatin dissolved in 1/4 c. water
1 (approximately 16 oz.) can asparagus bits, drained (*or* fresh cooked asparagus)
1 c. celery, chopped
1/2 c. pecans, chopped or halves
2 tbsp. pimientos, diced
1 tbsp. fresh lemon juice
2 tbsp. onion, minced
Salt and pepper

Simmer sugar, water, and vinegar in a small saucepan for 5 minutes. Add softened gelatin to hot liquid. Cover and refrigerate. When mixture begins to congeal, pour into an attractive glass serving bowl, add the other ingredients, and chill until firm. (The green asparagus and red pimientos in this shimmering, jewel-like congealed salad look especially festive at Christmastime.) This recipe will serve 7 or 8.[6]

## Aesthetics of Broccoli and Cauliflower

My husband and I recall that in our childhood broccoli and cauliflower were served cooked, plain and unadorned. However, as young adults we were delighted to find that these veggies could appear at the table all dressed up.

### Miss Southland Basic Broccoli

1 bunch of broccoli
¼ c. butter, melted
¼ c. fresh lemon juice

Trim off any large broccoli leaves, cut off the tough ends of the stalks, and wash the broccoli. If the stalks are larger than one inch in diameter, make lengthwise slits in them. Cook the broccoli, covered, in a small amount of boiling, salted water until just tender, around 12 to 15 minutes. Drain. Meanwhile, melt the butter, add the lemon juice, and mix well. Pour over the hot broccoli just prior to serving.

### "Say Cheese" Sauce for Broccoli

2 tbsp. vegetable oil
2 rounded tbsp. flour
¼ tsp. salt
1¼ c. milk
1 c. Cheddar cheese, grated
Enough cooked broccoli spears for 3 or 4 people

In a saucepan, warm the oil. Stir in the flour and salt, and cook until the mixture bubbles a bit. Stir in milk, whisking to remove all lumps. When the sauce is smooth and thickened, stir in cheese. Serve over hot broccoli. Yield: 3 or 4 servings.

## Tennessee Beauty Broccoli Bake

1 lg. head of fresh broccoli, cut up and steamed until just tender, or 2 (8-oz.) pkgs. frozen chopped broccoli *or* broccoli spears, cooked according to package directions
2 eggs, beaten
3/4 c. mayonnaise
1 to 2 c. Cheddar or American cheese, grated (depending upon your passion for cheese)
1 small onion, chopped
1 (10 1/2 oz.) can cream of mushroom soup

Wheat germ *or* Ritz cracker crumbs

Combine the first six ingredients. Spoon into a 1 1/2-quart casserole dish. Top with wheat germ or Ritz cracker crumbs. Bake at 350° F. for 45 minutes. Serves 6 to 8.[7]

## Alabama Strut Broccoli Salad

1/2 c. mayonnaise
3 tbsp. vinegar
2 tbsp. sugar

Mix and chill. Add:

2 bunches broccoli, chopped (8 c., mostly florets)
1 c. Cheddar cheese, shredded
1/2 c. onion, chopped
Imitation bacon bits *or* the real thing

Refrigerate 6 to 8 hours or overnight before serving.

## Miss Congeniality Cauliflower Salad

½ medium cauliflower
3 carrots, sliced diagonally
1 tsp. lemon juice
1 large green pepper, sliced into rings
1 medium onion, sliced into rings
½ c. white vinegar
½ tsp. dried oregano
⅓ c. oil
1 garlic clove, cut in half
2 tsp. sugar
¼ tsp. salt

Wash cauliflower thoroughly and separate into medium-sized flowerets. Pare carrots and slice diagonally. Place carrots and cauliflower in large saucepan with enough water to cover. Add 1 teaspoon lemon juice. Cook uncovered until vegetables are just tender but crisp, about 4 minutes. Drain. Place all vegetables in large plastic container, preferably one that can be inverted. Combine vinegar, oregano, oil, garlic, sugar, and salt. Pour over vegetables. Refrigerate overnight. If possible, invert container occasionally or stir vegetables so that all will be well-marinated. Drain vegetables to serve. Return leftover vegetables to marinade and store in refrigerator. Serves 6.[8]

## Comforting Cabbage

After the Civil War, Virginia soldier Isaac Coles recalled that as a nearly-starved prisoner of war he repeatedly had a "delightful, substantial, hunger-satisfying dream of cabbage and corn bread." Upon reflection, Coles thought it noteworthy that his subconscious fixation was on a meal prepared by and for the slaves on his family's plantation, rather than on the "delicacies of my father's table." [9]

Cabbage and other inexpensive vegetables seem to epitomize good, comforting, honest food.

A.L. "Tommie" Bass, a northeast Alabama herbalist, described his families' menus while he was growing up:

"The mid-day meal was the biggest. We'd often have soup, beans, potatoes, corn, cabbage. Sometimes there was meat." [10]

## Southern Slope Cabbage Wedges

½ medium head cabbage
1 to 2 tbsp. butter, melted
Salt and pepper

Remove any tough outer leaves from the cabbage, and cut into four wedges. Put water in a skillet to a depth of ½ inch. Bring to a boil, add a generous sprinkle of salt, and the cabbage wedges. Simmer, covered, 8 to 10 minutes, or until the cabbage is tender. Pour off any remaining water, and return to low heat until the moisture has evaporated. Add the butter, black pepper, and a little more salt if desired.

## Summer Respite Ice Box Slaw

Layer in a large heat-proof container:

1 medium cabbage, shredded
2 onions, thinly sliced

Heat together to boiling:

¾ c. sugar
1 tsp. celery seed
1 tsp. dry mustard
1 c. white vinegar
1 ½ tsp. salt
¾ c. salad oil

Pour the hot dressing over the layered cabbage and onions. Cover and refrigerate.[11]

# Smooth and Creamy Coleslaw

6 c. finely-shredded green cabbage
1/3 c. chopped onion
1/3 c. chopped cucumber
1 c. shredded carrots

Toss ingredients together. Prepare dressing:

2/3 c. mayonnaise *or* salad dressing
2 tbsp. sugar
2 tbsp. white vinegar
1 tbsp. milk
1/2 tsp. salt
1/8 tsp. paprika

Combine all dressing ingredients. Refrigerate for one hour before mixing with tossed cabbage, onion, cucumber and carrots.[12]

# Taste of Texas Coleslaw

1 medium cabbage, grated or shredded
1 medium green pepper, finely chopped
1 large onion, finely chopped
1 carrot, grated
1/2 c. salad oil
1/2 c. white vinegar
3/4 c. sugar
1 tsp. salt
1/2 tsp. dry mustard
2 tbsp. fresh parsley
1/4 tsp. black pepper

Toss vegetables lightly. Blend remaining ingredients until smooth. Combine. Cover. Refrigerate overnight. This coleslaw will keep 2 weeks refrigerated.[13]

Following is a recipe from over a century ago, when "organic" was the *only* type of gardening.

### "Cabbage Boiled with Bacon"

"Quarter a head of hard white cabbage, examine for insects, lay in salt and water several hours. An hour before dinner, drain and put in a pot in which bacon has been boiling — a pod of red pepper boiled with it will make it more wholesome and improve flavor of both bacon and cabbage." [14]

## All-Consumed Corn

Corn is foundational to Southern life. At the table, it is consumed on the cob or as cut-off kernels. If allowed to mature in the field, it can be ground into cornmeal. The grain is fed to hogs and chickens, and the sweet stalk, stored as silage, is a staple of the self-sufficient livestock farm. Ground corn also provides the mash for corn whiskey, which in its untaxed form has been a perennial illegal Southern cash crop.

With the next few recipes I will only attempt to represent corn as a vegetable on the table, leaving cornmeal for discussions in many of my other books.

Southerners like their corn on the cob freshly picked and eaten soon. In fact, the story goes that a particular farmer took a portable gas cooker out to the cornfield so that he could boil ears of corn without even removing them from the stalk![15]

### Summer Succulence Grilled Corn on the Cob

Medium-sized ears of corn

Open outer husks of corn and remove silks. Replace husks. Wrap tightly in aluminum foil. Place in hot coals or on grill and cook 15 to 20 minutes (or until tender). Remove foil and husks, and serve immediately with butter and salt if desired.

Note: If you want to do this without the foil, pull the husks back, remove the silks, and then close the husks and secure them in place with a wire twist-tie. Soak the ears of corn in cold water for several minutes. Remove and shake off the excess water. Bury the corn in hot ashes and coals of a campfire or fireplace or charcoal grill. Leave there for an hour. Check one ear for tenderness. If ready, remove the husks and enjoy.

## My Mama's Corn Pudding

2 c. corn (fresh or canned)
1/4 c. sugar
1/2 tsp. salt
Dash of pepper
1/2 c. milk
1/2 tsp. baking powder
2 tbsp. flour
1 egg, beaten

    Mix everything together and bake at 350° F. for 45 minutes. Yield: 4 servings.[16]

## Best-of-the-Patch Corn and Tomato Casserole

8 to 12 ears fresh corn (4 to 5 c. cut corn)
1/4 c. butter *or* bacon drippings
2 c. water
4 slices crisp cooked bacon, crumbled
1/2 tsp. salt, or to taste
2 large tomatoes, peeled and sliced

    Cut corn from cob. Melt fat in a skillet, and add the corn. Sauté lightly for about five minutes. Add the 2 c. water, the crumbled bacon, and salt. Stir everything together. Next, spoon some of this corn mixture into a greased casserole dish. Put a few tomato slices on top of the mixture. Continue making layers, ending with tomato slices on top. Bake uncovered 30 minutes in a 350° F. oven. Yield: 5 to 6 servings.

## Cob's Legion Fresh Corn Fritters

1/4 c. all-purpose flour
1 tsp. salt
1/2 tsp. baking powder
1 1/2 c. fresh corn, cut from cob
2 eggs, separated
1/4 tsp. black pepper
1 tbsp. vegetable oil
Shortening to a depth of 1/4 inch in frying pan

    Combine flour, salt, and baking powder. Beat yolks until light yellow and add all other ingredients except whites. Mix well. Beat whites into soft peaks and fold into corn mixture. Drop 1/4 cup dollops in hot shortening to fry.[17]

## The Long Lean String Bean

    In my childhood days in Virginia, the string bean was one of the most commonly-served green veggies. Mashed potatoes and string beans seemed to go hand-in-hand, so to speak. Most folks liked gravy or butter on the 'taters, but the snaps typically needed no enhancement because they were usually cooked with some cut of pork. (By the way, as you are probably already aware, we Southerners call green beans "string beans" or "snaps.") Snaps, unlike peas and many other food items, were thought to be just about as tasty after having been home-canned as they were if gathered fresh. After all, they were always long-cooked before they achieved their greasy-good ready-to-eat status.

    Some years ago Richmond, Virginia, was said to be "the green bean capital of the world," with a higher per capita consumption of string beans than anywhere else on Earth. The following recipe is representative of that era, combining snaps with also-popular limas and that handy 20th-century invention, cream of mushroom soup.

## Capital City Almond-Crowned Beans

1 (10 oz.) pkg. frozen cut green beans (*or* 1½ lbs. fresh green beans)
1 (10 oz.) pkg. frozen baby lima beans (*or* about 2 c. fresh limas, *or* 1 (16 to 17 oz.) can lima beans
1 (10½ oz.) can cream of mushroom soup
½ c. slivered almonds

Cook the fresh or frozen beans together in a small amount of boiling, salted water for 8 minutes. (Almost all of the water should cook away.) Stir in cream of mushroom soup. Pour into a baking dish and sprinkle with almonds. Bake at 350° F. for 50 minutes. Serves 6 to 8.


## Snaps Under Pressure

"In 4-qt. pressure cooker use 2 qts. (canned — without their own liquid, [or] fresh or frozen) string beans. Use 2 [inch] wedge cured salt pork, 1 tsp. salt, ½ tsp. sugar to ¼ c. water. Cook under pressure 45 minutes. Remove pan from heat until pressure goes down. Remove top; return to heat; cook & stir until all water is gone. Some like them scorched." [18]


## Southern - Style Pole Beans and New Potatoes

1 (½ lb.) ham hock *or* 4 slices fried bacon, crumbled
3 lb. fresh pole beans
1 medium onion, sliced crosswise (optional)
5 c. water
½ tsp. sugar (optional)
12 small new Irish potatoes
Salt and pepper

Put the ham hock or bacon in a large pot; bring to a boil, then reduce heat and simmer for an hour. Meanwhile, string the beans, and cut or snap into 1½-inch pieces.

After the pork has simmered for an hour, add the beans, onion if enjoyed, and sugar. Cook 1½ to 2 hours or until the beans shrivel, adding additional water if necessary. About 30 minutes before you plan to serve the beans, put in the potatoes and cook until the potatoes are tender, then season with salt and pepper.

## Quintessential Four Bean Salad

½ c. onion, chopped
½ c. celery, chopped
½ c. green pepper, chopped
1¾ c. (15½ oz.) string beans, canned or cooked
1¾ c. (15½ oz.) red kidney beans, canned or cooked
1¾ c. (15½ oz.) limas, canned or cooked
1¾ c. (15½ oz.) yellow wax beans, canned or cooked
1¾ c. (15½ oz.) whole kernel corn, canned or cooked
1⅓ c. sugar
1⅓ c. white vinegar
1 c. mild-flavored olive oil *or* vegetable oil
¼ tsp. black pepper
1 tsp. salt
Dash of crushed red pepper

Drain and rinse canned vegetables. Combine all ingredients. Chill overnight or longer. Drain off marinade before serving.

## North Carolina Bean Salad

2 c. fresh or frozen green peas, cooked; *or* 1 can (15½ oz.) small green peas
1 can (15½ oz.) red kidney beans
1 can (15½ oz.) yellow wax beans (or fresh)
1 can (15½ oz.) green beans (or fresh or frozen)
2 c. red cabbage, shredded
1 c. onion, chopped
3 tbsp. pimento, chopped

½ c. *each* oil, vinegar, *and* brown sugar
¾ tsp. salt

Drain and rinse canned beans. Combine all ingredients. Chill at least 6 to 8 hours.

# Lettuce, Pray

Most Southern meals begin with an invocation of Divine blessing, and many now follow with a first course invoking the refreshing texture of lettuce. Raw-vegetable salads offer infinite variety and spur-of-the-moment flexibility. The following favorite of our family requires a bit more advance preparation.

### Mrs. McGregor's Lettuce Salad

Dressing:
1 c. mayonnaise plus 2 tbsp. sugar *or* ½ c. *each* mayonnaise and Thousand Island dressing *or* 1 c. mayonnaise and 2 tbsp. Thousand Island dressing

1 (10 oz.) pkg. frozen green peas, uncooked (or fresh peas, blanched)
½ c. green pepper, chopped
1 medium onion, chopped
¼ c. imitation bacon bits (*or* 8 slices bacon, cooked, drained, and diced)
1 c. celery, chopped

4 hard-cooked eggs, sliced
½ head iceberg lettuce, torn into bite-sized pieces
1 c. (4 oz.) Cheddar cheese, grated

Mix together dressing. Sir in the next five ingredients. Cover and let chill 8 to 12 hours, then stir in lettuce and eggs. Spoon into an 8x8-inch glass dish. Sprinkle cheese on top. Cover and let chill an hour or so.

# The Sublime Subliminal Lima

When Henry and I were "getting serious" about each other, there were some meals eaten with each set of parents. We were rather young, so my parents were not too thrilled about our romance. Mother got it into her head (or did she?) that Henry's favorite menu was a Southern repast of pork chops, sweet potatoes, and limas. Actually, those were his *least*-enjoyed foods! She served that menu frequently — so frequently, in fact, that Henry eventually developed a strong liking for all those edibles (perhaps a Pavlovian response to pleasant associations?).

Here is Mrs. Samuel Tyree's advice on cooking limas, from over a century ago:

## "Lima Beans"

"Shell and throw into cold water. [Just before cooking, drain off water.] Put in boiling water an hour before dinner; add some salt; when tender, drain off the water and add a tablespoonful fresh butter. Beans are seldom cooked enough." [19]

Perhaps the lack of modern technology in Mrs. Tyree's kitchen would have prevented her from enjoying the following:

## Cool Breezes Lima Salad

1 (10 oz.) pkg. frozen limas (fresh is even better)
1 (10 oz.) pkg. frozen green peas (or fresh)
1 c. celery, thinly sliced
½ c. onion, chopped
Mayonnaise to moisten
Salt and pepper
1 small pkg. (3 oz.) cream cheese *or* Neufchâtel cheese, cubed

Prepare the limas and peas according to package directions. Drain and cool. When cool, add the remaining ingredients, chill, and serve.

# More Than Merely Mushrooms

According to a nostalgic encyclopedia of New Orleans food, the 1901 *Picayune Creole Cook Book*, "... the family that makes it a daily practice to eat vegetables and fruits, when in season ["in season" in New Orleans is practically all the time], will never have need of a physician."[20] Actually, South Louisiana's cooks have never needed an appeal to health in order to utilize fruits, vegetables, or any edible thing; sensual delight suffices!

Here is one of our favorite vegetable recipes from Louisiana. (Mushrooms are fungi, I know, but they seem sort of like vegetables when they are served!)

## Louisiana Mushroom Casserole

Henry and I lived in New Orleans for four years, and our hearts still belong to "The City that Care Forgot." One of our best friends there was Aubrey Jenkins. One Christmas when we were back in Louisiana for a visit, Aubrey took us to Christmas dinner at his parents' home in Hammond. What a spectacular spread awaited us! His mom, Beatrice, or Bea B., as she is affectionately called, and Aubrey's step-dad, Curtis, served us outstanding Cajun/Creole cuisine combined with lovin' Southern hospitality. Star attractions on the "groaning board" were roasted turkey tails (a local specialty) and Bea's out-of-this-world Louisiana Mushroom Casserole.

\* \* \*

1 lb. fresh mushrooms
8 slices of bacon, cooked, drained, and crumbled
$1/2$ c. onion, chopped
$1/2$ c. celery, chopped
$1/2$ c. bread crumbs
$1/2$ c. mayonnaise
1 tsp. soy sauce
$1/2$ tsp. salt (or less, to suit taste)

A sprinkling of chopped fresh parsley *or* dried parsley flakes
1 c. Cheddar cheese, grated

Rinse the mushrooms in salted water. Rinse 3 or 4 times and drain well. Cut off stems and chop up. If the mushrooms are extremely large, cut them in half. Meanwhile, sauté the onions and celery in some of the bacon grease. Mix mushrooms, bacon, onion, celery, bread crumbs, mayonnaise, soy sauce, salt, and parsley. Spoon half of this mixture into a baking dish and cover with ½ c. cheese. Put the balance of the mixture over this layer and top with ½ cup cheese. Bake at 350° F. for about 30 minutes. Yield: 6 to 8 servings.

## Summer-Sensing Okra

My husband Henry recalls from his childhood that, in their Southside Virginia garden, okra was the plant most forgiving of extreme heat and drought. Once hot weather stimulated the seeds into fast-growing little okra "trees," a new crop of mucilaginous seed pods could be gathered almost every day. His family enjoyed their okra prepared in a mild Upper-South version of gumbo, a well-known signature dish of the Gulf Coast. Another Deep-South use of okra follows:

### Creole Okra

2 tbsp. bacon drippings *or* vegetable oil
½ c. onion, chopped
½ c. bell (or green) pepper, chopped
3 c. sliced okra
3 c. tomatoes, chopped
1 tbsp. sugar
¼ c. chopped fresh parsley
Salt and pepper to taste

Sauté the onion and green pepper in the fat until tender. Add okra; cook over medium heat for 5 minutes, stirring constantly. Add the remaining ingredients, and simmer, uncovered for 15 minutes. (Add a little water if necessary.) Serves 4.

## Of Onions and Spring

An early and certain sign of spring in the Southern garden is the vivid green of the restorative fresh spring onion. Here is a Civil War-era recipe (which reminds me vaguely of Egg Foo Yung!), followed by two others of much later origin.

### Fried Spring Onions

"Wash and chop 2 dozen spring onions (tops and bottoms). Put bacon grease in pan. Add water if needed and a little sugar. Cover and steam until tender (and water is almost gone). Then break an egg in it and stir around to solidify it enough to serve." [21]

### Simply Nice Green Rice

3/4 c. green onions, thinly sliced
3 tbsp. vegetable oil
1 c. white rice, uncooked
1/2 c. green peppers, minced
1/4 c. fresh parsley, minced
2 c. chicken broth
1/2 to 1 tsp. salt, or much less if the chicken broth is salty
Pepper to taste

Cook onions (use tops as well as white part) in oil until soft but not browned. Add remaining ingredients. Pour into a 2-quart casserole dish with a lid. (If no cover is available, use aluminum foil.) Bake in 350° F. oven about 30 minutes, or until rice is tender. Toss lightly with a fork before serving. Serves 6.[22]

## Favorite Things Salad

1 pkg. frozen mixed vegetables, cooked until just tender, drained and chilled (add some limas if not included in the package)
½ c. onion, chopped
⅓ c. green pepper, chopped
⅓ c. celery, chopped
2 tbsp. sweet pickle, chopped
2 tbsp. pimientos, chopped
½ c. mozzarella *or* Cheddar cheese, cubed
Salt to taste
1 tbsp. plain yogurt
1 tbsp. mayonnaise

    Combine everything and chill.

## The Honorable Black-Eyed Pea

    During the Civil War, Confederate soldiers often found themselves consuming cowpeas, also known as cornfield peas or black-eyed peas. So dependent upon that food source were they that, even years after the surrender, General Robert E. Lee stated that he never passed a field of cowpeas without feeling that he should stop and salute.[23]

### "Cornfield or Black Eye Peas"

    "Shell early in the morning, throw into water till an hour before dinner, when put into boiling water, covering close while cooking. Add a little salt, just before taking from the fire. Drain and serve with a large spoonful fresh butter, or put in a pan with a slice of fat meat, and simmer a few minutes. Dried peas must be soaked overnight, and cooked twice as long as fresh." [24]

## "Recipe for Cooking Cornfield Peas"

"Gather your peas 'bout sun-down. The following day, 'bout eleven o'clock, gorge out your peas with your thumb nail. . . . Rinse your peas, parboil them, then fry 'em with some several slices of streaked middling, encouraging of the gravy to seep out and intermarry with your peas. When moderately brown, but not scorched, empty into a dish. Mash 'em gently with a spoon, mix with raw tomatoes sprinkled with a little brown sugar and the immortal dish [is] quite ready. Eat a heap. Eat more and more. It is good for your general health of mind and body. It fattens you up, makes you sassy, goes through and through your very soul. But why don't you eat? Eat on. By Jings. Eat. Stop? Never, while there is a pee [pea] in the dish." [25]

## Outstanding Dried Black-Eyed Peas

1 lb. dried black-eyed peas
1 tsp. salt
1 clove garlic, minced
½ c. bacon drippings *or* vegetable oil
3 cloves garlic, minced
3 medium-size green peppers, chopped
3 medium onions, cubed
2 bay leaves, pulverized
3 tbsp. vinegar
Salt and black pepper to taste

Pick over peas; wash thoroughly. Place in a heavy saucepan and cover with water; soak overnight.

Drain peas, and return to saucepan; cover with fresh boiling water. Add salt and one minced garlic clove; cover and simmer 3 hours, adding boiling water as needed.

Just before serving, heat bacon drippings in skillet; add the other three garlic cloves, green pepper, onion, and bay leaves. Cook until vegetables are tender. Stir in vinegar, salt, and pepper. Spoon into cooked peas; mix well. Yield: 8 to 10 servings.

# Soothing Potatoes

In an article entitled "50's Food" in an 1989 magazine, the writer exclaims, "Why, bellying up to a bowl of buttery mashed potatoes was like a mother's kiss!" [26]

## Gravy-Sopping Mashed Potatoes

8 medium-size potatoes (about 3 1/2 lbs.), peeled and quartered
1/4 c. butter
1/2 to 1 c. milk, heated
1/2 tsp. salt (or to taste)
Dash of black pepper

Place potatoes in water to cover. Bring to a boil, reduce heat, cover and simmer 20 minutes or until the potatoes are fork-tender. Drain off the water. Mash with a potato masher; add butter, and enough milk to make the potatoes the consistency you like. Season to taste with salt and pepper. Serve with gravy, if desired.

## ". . . Variety in the Diet . . ."

In his *Kinfolks and Custard Pie*, Tennessean Walter N. Lambert declared, "I grew up believing that variety in the diet meant beans and potatoes one day and potatoes and beans the next." [27] Following are some recipes for Mr. Lambert (and other interested parties), the first of which dates from around 1879.

## "To Boil Irish Potatoes"

"Old potatoes must be nicely peeled and dropped in boiling water, covered with a lid and boiled hard half an hour. Then drain off the water and set by the fire. This makes them mealy." [28]

# Neatly Parsleyed New Potatoes

8 very small new potatoes
Water
1 tbsp. butter
Salt and freshly ground black pepper
¼ c. chopped fresh parsley

Put the well-scrubbed potatoes on a rack or trivet in a pot of steaming water. Bring the water beneath the potatoes to a boil, reduce heat, cover, and steam about 10 or 15 minutes or until the potatoes are tender when tested with a fork. (If you are not ready to serve the potatoes at this time, remove the pot from the stove and tip the pot lid.) Just before serving, toss the potatoes with the butter, salt, pepper, and parsley.

# Flatlanders' Pan-Fried Potatoes

Cut 4 medium-sized potatoes into ¼-inch-thick slices. Melt 3 tbsp. butter or other fat over medium heat in a large skillet. Add the potatoes. Cook 20 minutes or until tender, turning them occasionally.

# Old-Fashioned Cheese-Scalloped Potatoes

4 c. thinly sliced potatoes
1 tbsp. butter
¼ c. chopped onion
1 tbsp. all-purpose flour
½ tsp. salt (or to suit taste)
1⅔ c. milk
½ c. Cheddar cheese, grated

Boil potatoes until almost tender; drain. Melt butter, add onions, sauté briefly; then add flour, salt, and milk, stirring until thickened. Stir in cheese. Put the potatoes in a buttered casserole dish, pour on the thickened sauce, and bake at 350° F. for 30 minutes.

Note: Southerners seem to like anything scalloped. Cabbage, for example, is another vegetable which can benefit from a blanket of cream ("white") sauce.

## Not-Much-Trouble Scalloped Potatoes

6 or 7 medium-size potatoes, peeled and sliced
Onions, minced, if you desire
1 (10½ oz.) can cream of mushroom *or* cream of chicken soup
½ c. milk
1 c. Cheddar cheese, grated (optional)
Salt and pepper

Put part of the sliced potatoes in a large Pyrex dish. Mix the soup and milk together. Pour some of the soup mixture over the potatoes. Sprinkle on some of the cheese, if wanted. Repeat the layers until the ingredients are all used up. Sprinkle the top with salt and pepper. Bake at 350° F. for 1½ hrs. or until the potatoes are tender. (For a shortcut, boil the sliced potatoes first, and then proceed, baking only 30 minutes.)

## Portly Potatoes

There are many recipes for stuffed potatoes; creativity can have free rein. Here, however, is a fine example for gilding the commonplace potato. To further enhance the recipe, use "real" bacon, crumbled up, and "real" butter. — These are delicious!

\* \* \*

4 baking potatoes
¼ c. bacon bits
2 tbsp. onion, grated
⅔ c. warm milk
½ c. butter *or* margarine, melted
¼ tsp. salt
⅛ tsp. black pepper
½ c. Cheddar cheese, grated

Bake potatoes at 375° F. for about 1 hour. Cut in half and scoop the potato out of the skins. Mash the potatoes and add other ingredients, except cheese. Mix well and stuff into six to eight of the halves. Heat for 10 minutes at 375° F. Top with cheese and return to the oven until the cheese is melted. Also, please note that you may reduce the amount of milk called for, and add ½ c. cream of mushroom soup instead, for a different flavor.[29]

### Chill-Out Potato Salad

4 c. potatoes, cooked and diced
4 hard-cooked eggs, chopped
2 tbsp. prepared yellow mustard
2 tbsp. mayonnaise
1 tbsp. vinegar
¼ c. cucumber pickles, chopped
1 green pepper, chopped
¼ c. onion, chopped

    Mix gently with a fork.

## Garden Greens

    The following recipes demonstrate several exciting possibilities from the greens section of the garden (or market).

### Family Spinach Salad

1½ lbs. fresh spinach
½ lb. bacon
3 hard-cooked eggs

Italian dressing

    Wash and drain spinach thoroughly. Fry bacon until crisp, drain and crumble. Dice hard-cooked eggs. Toss together all ingredients. Serve with Italian dressing.

## Southern Lady's Creamed Spinach

2 lb. spinach
1 small onion, chopped
1½ tbsp. butter *or* margarine
¼ c. evaporated milk
½ tsp. salt, or to taste

Wash the spinach thoroughly, remove any tough stems, and cook until tender. Drain any excess water. Cook the onion in the butter until soft but not browned. Chop the spinach very fine. Add the onion, milk, and salt to the spinach and mix thoroughly. A dash of nutmeg may be added if desired. Reheat and serve. Serves 6.


## Turnip Greens with Cornmeal Dumplings

2 lbs. fresh turnip greens (*or* kale, mustard greens, spinach, *or* other greens of your choice)
Water
¼ lb. salt pork, ham, *or* bacon, chopped
Salt to taste

¾ c. self-rising cornmeal
1 egg, beaten
¼ c. milk
1 tbsp. vegetable oil

Wash greens thoroughly; cover with cold, salted water and let soak 1 hour; drain. Bring 2 cups of water to a boil; add greens and pork and return to a boil. Cover, reduce heat, and simmer 1 hour or more or until greens are very tender. Add salt to taste.

Combine cornmeal, egg, milk, and oil. Drop batter by teaspoonfuls on top of simmering greens. Cover and simmer 20 minutes longer. Makes 6 servings.

### Southern Classic Turnip Salad Greens

"Wash and stem tender leaves (approximately a 'sink full'). Bring a 2 to 3 gal. container half full of water to boil. Add ½ cup bacon grease, 2 tsp. salt, ½ tsp. soda (helps tenderize and keep green). Stir in salad with slotted spoon. Reduce heat, cook with top on, stirring frequently. Cook 10 to 15 minutes. To see if salad is done, take up a little and if it cuts tender, serve." [30]

## Prodigious Squash

Squash vines, like many other vegetables in the Southern garden, can produce almost outrageously during the peak of their season. For several years my husband and I harvested seemingly endless quantities of bright yellow baby crookneck summer squash. Our confidence as gardeners knew no bounds. Unfortunately, other critters also knew no bounds. It all seemed to happen at once: deer and groundhogs, greedy in general; and cutworms, a specific nemesis of squash. Ah, the joys and challenges of a gardener's life!

### Home Kitchen Squash

Summer squash is good cooked like this: Sauté some chopped-up onion in a little fat (oil, butter, bacon grease, your choice) in a skillet. Add thinly sliced squash, cover, and cook slowly until tender. Stir occasionally.

A 19th-century recipe reads like this:

### "To Stew Cymlings (or Squash, as it is sometimes called)."

"Peel and boil till tender. Run through a colander. To a pint of pulp, add one half pint rich milk, a heaping tablespoonful fresh butter and a little salt. Stew till thick like marmalade.

Pepper freely, pour over it, if convenient, half teacup cream, and serve." [31]

## Ritzy Company Squash Casserole

1½ pounds squash, cooked and mashed
1 (10½ oz.) can cream of chicken soup
¼ c. milk
¼ c. onion, chopped or grated
Salt and pepper to taste
Butter
Cheese Ritz crackers, crumbled

Mix ingredients with a small amount of cheese Ritz cracker crumbs, and then top with more crumbs and butter bits. Cook at 325° F. for 30 minutes. Serves 4 to 6.

## Savory Summer Squash

4 slices bacon, diced
6 c. summer squash, cut into ¼ inch slices
½ tsp. salt (or less to suit taste)
⅛ tsp. black pepper
2 tbsp. grated Parmesan cheese

Fry bacon in skillet until crisp. Drain on absorbent paper. Combine squash, salt and pepper in bacon drippings in skillet. Cover and cook, stirring occasionally, about 15 to 20 minutes, until tender. Just before serving, sprinkle with bacon and cheese.

## Church Supper Squash

2 lbs. squash (fresh or frozen)
2 tbsp. butter
1 lg. onion, chopped
3 tomatoes, peeled and chopped (whole canned tomatoes may be used)
⅓ c. sour cream *or* unflavored yogurt

2 tbsp. grated Cheddar cheese
Salt and pepper to taste

Dice unpeeled squash and cook in a small amount of water until tender. (If using frozen squash, cook according to package directions.) Drain off any remaining water. Sauté onion in butter until tender. Add tomatoes, squash, and half of the sour cream. Cook gently 10 minutes, then stir in cheese and the rest of the sour cream. Season to taste with salt and pepper.[32]

## Happy Discovery Yellow Squash

4 medium-size yellow squash, sliced
2 to 4 tbsp. butter
$1/2$ c. onion, chopped
2 hard-cooked eggs, chopped
$1/2$ c. Cheddar cheese, grated
1 c. buttered cracker crumbs

Cook the squash in a small amount of boiling, salted water for around 15 minutes or until just tender. Drain. Meanwhile, sauté the onion in butter until translucent. Combine all ingredients except the crumbs. Spoon into a lightly greased 1-qt. casserole dish. Sprinkle on the cracker crumbs. Bake uncovered at 350° F. for 15 to 20 minutes. Serves 4 to 6.

# "Long" Or Sweet Potatoes

Marion Cabell Tyree gives instructions for possible ways to serve boiled sweet potatoes according to the taste of diners in the 1800's.

## "To Boil Sweet Potatoes"

"Boil large, smooth potatoes till quite done. Peel and slice lengthwise. Pour melted butter over them. Some persons like a dressing of pepper, salt, butter, and cream. Others prefer butter, sifted sugar, and grated nutmeg." [33]

## Southern Sensations Fried Sweet Potatoes

Sweet potatoes, peeled and thinly sliced
Salt and pepper
Butter

    Melt butter in a frying pan. Add potatoes, sprinkling lightly with salt and generously with pepper. Sauté until the potatoes are tender and delicately browned.

## Big Orange Mashed Sweet Potatoes

3 large oranges, cut in half
1 tbsp. grated orange rind
1 tbsp. sugar
$1/4$ c. milk *or* orange juice
2 c. mashed sweet potatoes
$1/2$ tsp. cinnamon *or* $1/4$ tsp. nutmeg (or both)
Dash of salt
2 tbsp. butter, melted
1 additional tbsp. butter

    Scoop the pulp out of the orange halves. Scallop the edges of the scooped out orange shells by making V-shaped cuts with a sharp knife. Measure $1/3$ c. of drained pulp and blend with the remaining ingredients (except for the 1 extra tbsp. butter). Beat together the ingredients until smooth and fluffy. Fill the orange shells with the potato mixture. Dot the tops with the remaining butter. Bake at 350° F. for 25 to 30 minutes.

## How Sweet They Are!

    In an article entitled "The Gospel of Great Southern Food," Denise Gee remarks that renowned chef and cookbook writer Edna Lewis " . . . shudders at the idea of . . . marshmallows atop sweet potatoes." [34] (You will note that the next recipe, though sweet to the taste, uses no marshmallows!)

## Cousin Kathy's Sweet Potato Casserole

3 c. sweet potatoes, cooked and mashed (approximately 5 potatoes, depending upon size)
½ tsp. cinnamon
½ tsp. nutmeg
½ c. sugar
½ tsp. salt
2 eggs, beaten
½ stick butter *or* margarine, melted
½ c. milk
1 tsp. vanilla

Combine the above ingredients and spread into a greased 9x13x2-inch Pyrex baking dish. Mix together the following topping ingredients and spoon over the potato mixture:

⅓ c. butter or margarine, melted
1 c. brown sugar, packed
½ c. all-purpose flour
1 c. pecans, finely chopped

Bake at 350° F. for 45 minutes.[35]

## A Vegetable By Any Other Name

Nothing could be finer than a homegrown, vine-ripened tomato. (Oh, yes, I know that the tomato is technically a "fruit," but doesn't everyone think of and serve it as a — America's favorite, they say — vegetable?) If you can't wait for them to get ripe, or if a fall frost threatens your crop, you can make the following dish. You will notice that, in these instructions, specific amounts of most ingredients are left up to the cook's discretion.

## Green Tomato Casserole

"Slice 4 green medium-sized tomatoes into $1/4$-inch slices. Butter a 5-cup baking dish and start with tomatoes topped with salt, pepper, (if desired) sugar, grated cheese and buttered bread crumbs. Repeat process and bake covered 1 hour at 400° [F.]. Remove cover to brown cheese." [36]


The next recipe is from the 1879 *Housekeeping in Old Virginia*, compiled before professional cookbook writers listed specific, standardized measurements for ingredients. (Fannie Farmer was a trend-setter in her use of concise measurements and step-by-step instructions.[37] Her book, *The Boston Cooking-School Cook Book*, was first published in 1896.)

## "Stewed Tomatoes"

"Scald and peel the tomatoes, chop fine, season with salt, pepper, onion, and a little sugar. Put in some pieces of buttered light [yeast] bread, cut up very fine. Add a lump of butter, and stew in a saucepan." [38]


## Heavenly Halves Broiled Tomato Cups

6 tomatoes
$1/2$ c. sour cream
$1/2$ c. mayonnaise
$1/4$ c. grated Parmesan cheese
1 tsp. garlic salt
2 tbsp. fresh lemon juice
1 tbsp. chopped fresh parsley
3 green onions, minced

Cut tomatoes in half crosswise. Combine remaining ingredients, blending well. Top each tomato half with some of the mixture. Broil tomatoes until bubbly. Makes 12 servings.

## Cousin Tinky's Tomato Cheese Dumplings

2 c. canned or home-cooked tomatoes, chopped
1 tbsp. sugar
3/4 tsp. salt
1 tbsp. butter
1/4 tsp. black pepper
1/4 tsp. dried basil

**Dumplings:**

1 c. flour (whole wheat preferred)
1 tbsp. baking powder
3/4 tsp. salt
1 tbsp. vegetable oil
1/3 c. iced water

3/4 c. American cheese, grated

In a saucepan combine the first group of ingredients. Heat. Meanwhile, prepare the dumplings by combining the dry ingredients. Next add the oil and water, stirring until the dough begins to swell. Drop the dumplings by the spoonful into the boiling tomato mixture. Cover tightly and reduce heat; cook gently for 10 minutes. Spoon cooked dumplings into a warmed broiler-proof dish. Add 3/4 c. grated American cheese to tomato mixture in saucepan. Increase heat and cook 1 minute. Pour over dumplings. Run under hot broiler until bubbly. Yield: 4 to 6 servings.[39]

## Pick of the Patch Tomato-Herb Salad

2 to 3 large tomatoes, peeled (if desired), and chopped
1/2 tsp. minced fresh basil
1/2 tsp. minced fresh marjoram
1/4 c. plain French (vinaigrette) dressing
Lettuce

Combine herbs and dressing. Place tomatoes on lettuce leaves on individual plates. Pour dressing mixture over tomatoes.

4. Recipe courtesy the author's mother, Reba J. Beaver, Chatham, Virginia.
5. *Ibid.*
6. Recipe courtesy Lyon M. Fraune, Washington, North Carolina.
7. Recipe courtesy Evelyn Helvey, Johnson City, Tennessee.
8. *Educated Cooks*, Chatham, Virginia, ca. 1980, pp. 8-9, recipe contributed by Faye Peery.
9. Maud Carter Clement, *War Recollections of the Confederate Veterans of Pittsylvania County*, Rawley Martin Chapter, United Daughters of the Confederacy, Chatham, Virginia, 1961, pp. 74-75.
10. John K. Crellin, ed., *Plain Southern Eating: From the Reminiscences of A.L. "Tommie" Bass, Herbalist*, Duke University Press, Durham, North Carolina, 1988, p. 16.
11. Adapted from a recipe by Nancy Crawley Shelton, *Idle Hens Don't Lay*, Woodlawn Academy, Chatham, Virginia, 1976, p. 141.
12. Recipe courtesy Kitty Doss, *Educated Cooks*, p. 9.
13. Adapted from a recipe by Alice L. Shelton, *Tasting Luncheon Recipes: May 26, 1979*, sponsored by Watson Memorial United Methodist Women, Chatham, Virginia.
14. Tyree, p. 251.
15. *Come On In! Recipes from the Junior League of Jackson, Mississippi*, published by the Junior League of Jackson, Jackson, Mississippi, 1991, p. 141.
16. Reba J. Beaver.
17. Recipe courtesy Jodie D. Sullivan, Gretna, Virginia.
18. *Idle Hens Don't Lay*, p. 21, recipe contributed by Mary Jac Easley Meadows.
19. Tyree, p. 245.
20. *The Picayune's Creole Cook Book*, Second Edition, *The Picayune*, New Orleans, Louisiana, 1901, p. 205.
21. *Idle Hens Don't Lay*, p. 21, recipe contributed by Adelaide Dugger.
22. *Miss Fluffy's Rice Cook Book*, Rice Council, Houston, Texas, circa 1970, p. 29.
23. *A Catalogue of the South*, Oxmoor House, Birmingham, Alabama, 1974, p. 63.
24. Tyree, p. 254.
25. *Ibid.*, pp. 253-254, recipe attributed to Mozis Addums.
26. Linda Dillon, "50's Food," *1,001 Home Ideas*, August 1989, p. 95.
27. Walter N. Lambert, *Kinfolks and Custard Pie*, University of Tennessee Press, Knoxville, Tennesee, 1989, p. 146.
28. Tyree, p. 246.
29. Recipe courtesy Mary Gail Easley, Chatham, Virginia.
30. *Idle Hens Don't Lay*, p. 24, recipe contributed by Jessie Moore Easley.
31. Tyree, pp. 240-241.
32. Adapted from a recipe provided by Nilla Tredway, Chatham, Virginia.
33. Tyree, p. 248.
34. Denise Gee, "The Gospel of Great Southern Food," *Southern Living*, June 1996, Birmingham, Alabama, p. 128.
35. Recipe courtesy Kathy B. Marlow, Kannapolis, North Carolina.
36. *Idle Hens Don't Lay*, p. 21, recipe contributed by Mrs. W.B. Crawley.
37. Patrick Dunne and Charles L. Mackie, "Cookery Books," *Historic Preservation*, vol. 42, no. 3, May/June 1990, p. 59.
38. Tyree, p. 244.
39. Recipe courtesy Marguerite C. Gunn, Radford, Virginia.
40. *Queen Anne's Table Cookbook*, Edenton Historical Commission, Edenton, North Carolina, p. 41.

(Note: fresh thyme, rosemary, or savory, or a combination of herbs may be substituted.)

## Edenton Tomato Aspic

2½ c. (20 oz.) canned tomatoes
1 c. celery, chopped
½ c. onion, chopped
½ c. green pepper, chopped
½ tsp. salt
1 tbsp. sugar
Sprinkling of black pepper
3 tbsp. vinegar
1 pkg. (3 oz.) lemon Jell-O

Boil tomatoes, celery, onion, and green pepper for two minutes. Add salt, sugar, pepper, vinegar. Pour mixture over the lemon Jell-O powder, stirring to dissolve. Pour into an appropriate dish. Let congeal.[40]

## Conclusion

Flavor, color, health benefits — what's not to love about vegetables? Eat up.

## Notes

1. *The Southern Heritage Vegetables Cookbook*, Oxmoor House, Birmingham, Alabama, 1983, p. 59.
2. *Mrs. Beeton's Cookery Book*, Ward, Lock & Co., Ltd., London, 1902, p. 20.
3. Marion Cabell Tyree, editor, *Housekeeping in Old Virginia*, John P. Morton and Company, Louisville, Kentucky, 1879, p. 238.